SPELLS AGAINST *the* DARKNESS

VERSES OF QUIET MAGIC

RODERICK MACDONALD

Pownal Street Press

CHARLOTTETOWN

pownal
street
press

www.pownalstreetpress.com

Spells Against the Darkness: Verses of Quiet Magic. Edited by Danielle Loewen & Mo Duffy. Proofread by Alison Strumberger. Cover and interior design by Jordan Beaulieu. The text was set in Garamond Premier Pro.

Cataloging data available by Library and Archives Canada.
ISBN 978-1-998129-57-7 | E-book ISBN: 978-1-998129-58-4

Pownal Street Press gratefully acknowledges Mi'kma'ki, the ancestral and unceded territory of the Mi'kmaq First Nation on whose land our office is located.

The publisher acknowledges the support of the Government of Prince Edward Island.

Printed and bound in Canada.

1 2 3 4 5 25 26 27 28 29

For Mike and Dan

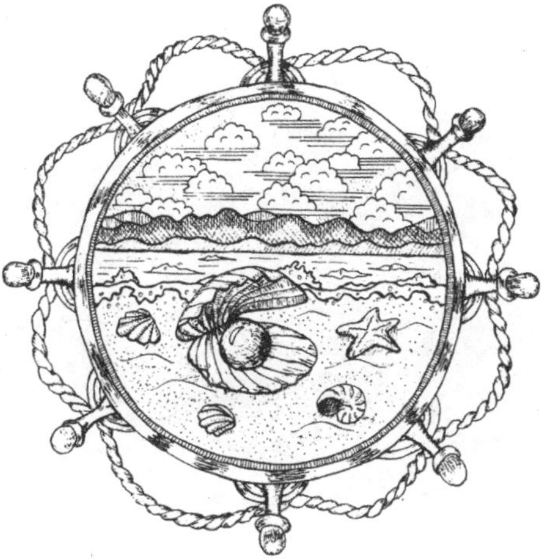

Spells for Joy

SNOW BUNTINGS

They explode from frozen fields
And the snowbird galaxy whirls
Rippling music sounds
Feathers gleam like pearls

The diurnal moon hangs, misplaced
A melancholy ghost
While above the withered rye stalks
Soars this cheerful host

Icy peaks of mud protrude
Winter's broken teeth
And wind-borne snow lies heavy
Upon the blueberry heath

Still the ghost-moon oversees
From a washed-out sky
This wasteland dead and brittle
Yet, the snowbirds fly

They fly as if to Heaven
Not in frigid air below
As if to conjure paradise
A wish can make it so

STARS IN THE RIVER

The wind was calm, the river shone with light
Reflections of the spheres and stars on high
And in the east the dawn then chased the night
A bright horizon strip that cut the sky
The water constellations drew me down
Until I swam, suspended in the deep
There, in the starry coldness would I drown
In dazzling numbness find my final sleep
A breath! A rising breeze then touched the stream
And broke the spell that wily night had cast
I stood as if awakened from a dream
Beneath the morning sky, empty and vast
The silken night's reflections can deceive
And lucky men are granted a reprieve

FROM THE BAR

Claret

Enchanted
Sun's radiance bottled
Poured with a delicious murmur
A flavour suffused
With the hopes of spring
And the joys of fall harvests
I recall the halcyon seasons
And dream, beguiled

Ale

Drink of weight
The vanguard of fermentation
Bearing the banner of civilization
Robust companion, heavy in my glass
Your hoppy perfume floats
Where good times pass

Martini

Alchemy of gin and vermouth
Dirty, with clouded brine
And dancing olive
With aroma evocative
Of fall leaves when long nights begin
And our souls swim
In pools of misty memory

LIFE OF EASE

I may lack gainful employment
However, I'm focused on full-time enjoyment
I didn't punch in
But the work is done
Now, I'll sit in the sun

Some people choose to vie and contest
I'll enjoy an unearned rest
Didn't enter the race
Somehow I won
Think I'll sit in the sun

I could seek to enhance my station
Run the village or lead the nation
I'm elected
Although I didn't run
I'll sit in the sun

Should I live with stress and care
Or wear out the seat of my easy chair?
Troubles all over
I have none
Here in the sun

Time runs short; I ask you, please
Join me in this life of ease
Don't stay in the shadow
Come have some fun
Sit with me in the sun

SUMMER STORY

Write a summer story
Etch it with sandy toes
Punctuate with ice cream
Adorn it with a rose

Bathe in guilt-free pleasure
In conscience-melting sun
Seize the glistening treasure
Responsible to none

Truth is just a story
And cares are washed away
For sin's absolved
Nothing's resolved
Listlessness reigns
Throughout the lazy day

ST. PATRICK'S DAY

Annual Irish weave
In an ocean of green plastic
As the evening turns fantastic
While the barman grins
In an Irish mist
Which swirls and spins

And I
In a trance
See the leprechauns start to dance

The manic, terpsichorean clan
Launch into the Running Man
Back and forth, they stamp their boots
Emitting piercing, impish hoots
They spring and roll with such precision
And demonstrate the fifth position
Breaking from this grand design
They form a tiny Conga Line

Not content with this commotion
Now they dance The Locomotion
I laugh, and laugh, and stare wide-eyed
As they begin The Electric Slide

Then each sprite
Becomes an emerald point of light
Like bright green moths they fly and spread
In circles all around my head

They're real! The People do exist
They live inside an Irish mist

FOLLY BRIDGE IN THE FOG

The fog paints shimmering twilight on the day
At Folly Bridge, where cold air meets the stream
We step into this otherworld of grey
And give our senses over to the dream
We smell the dampness of the ancient stones
Our mingled sweet, soft breath hangs in a cloud
The heavy, clinging droplets chill our bones
While ghostly fibres wrap us in a shroud
We walk together through this shadowland
As River Isis measures time below
In muffled stillness there, I take your hand
Lit by the haloed streetlights' waxy glow
I will remember walking in this mist
When cold October air and Isis kissed

MORNING LOVE SONG

Grey lumps of oatmeal crawl into my bowl
From the pot to which they cling
No amount of sugar and milk
Can disguise this glutenous thing

Bread mourns for its cremated kin
The smoke alarm sounds the last post
The kitchen chokes in a bluish pall
As I scrape soot from the toast

Eggs slide on the greasy ooze
Victims of a crime
Translucent albumen shivers
And weeps into the slime

In the unfathomable jam jar
Relics defy description
An archeological trove
To baffle a dietitian

The tea is tepid and bitter
A most insipid brew
But this is a perfect breakfast
For, across the table is... you!

VIGIL

We watch the pale moon rise
It climbs above the trees
And joy within us flies

Leaves rattle in the breeze
Clouds chase past the moon
We feel our hearts' release

A star shines in the gloom
Night winds chill the air
Evening flowers bloom

I reach to stroke your hair
But I am just a ghost
Of me, you're unaware

Joy within us flies
We watch the pale moon rise

THE BOOKSHELF

Heroes and villains fight in the service
Of alien tzars
And good is triumphant in Edgar Rice Burroughs'
A Princess of Mars

Erudition and wit leap from the pages
Like a fountain has sprung
And we forgive Bryson his swank
In *The Mother Tongue*

I laugh at the antics of dubious folk
From castles and hovels
And enjoy the respite of Professor Leacock's
Bizarre *Nonsense Novels*

I idle and laze in the meter and rhyme
Penned where the tropic sea gleams
Seduced by the music to feel what is real
In Dennis' *Island of Dreams*

I breathe misty air and feel rising joy
At a new day begun
Eternally hopeful while watching Chris Yates
Casting at the Sun

When I close this book, and my head rests
On velveteen pillows
Soft, in my coffin place Kenneth Grahame's
The Wind in the Willows

THE LOBSTER

How mighty the lobster!
He thrashes his tail
And crashes the surf
Against sand dune and shale

He bellows in rage
And gnashes his teeth
While frightened crabs tremble
Inside the reef

Eight armoured legs stamp
And the sea floor will quake
There's no place to cower
For flounder or hake

His terrible claws
Lunge out at the skies
To pinch at the moon
Unaware, as she flies

Yes, mighty the lobster
A prince of a beast
And fortunate they
Who are called to his feast

ONE MORE CAST

I saw the sunrise, all aglow
Many happy hours ago
And cast my line below the hill
Where the pond lies, calm and still
Morning shimmered in dewy guise
I watched the speckled trout arise
And while the noon hour came and went
The air hung heavy with wildflower scent
The latter hours shone bright and passed
Until gentle evening came at last
A full day since I made my start
I pack my bag with grateful heart
I see the sunset, all aglow
Just one more cast before I go

LAUNDRY

One with the piled laundry, you dance your way
Between the wild strawberry vines
On this windy, perfect drying day
Your dress blows and the sun shines
And your hips curve into the basket's design

Sheets smell of the sky and sea
As we lie in eloquent hush and reverie

NIGHT LIGHTS

All are inside now
I'm alone with the night
Embers glow and die
They tumble in my sight

The fire folds the air
Into a translucent cloak
Angel sparks ascend
On a stairway of smoke

In the darkling pines
Fireflies flash and soar
With fairy lamps they signal
In sexual semaphore

Lights blink, dead, across the field
As the darkness grows

Empty eyes: the strings of bulbs
That lit the patios

The streetlight stands its vigil
At the corner of the lane
And bravely pushes back the night
As twilight starts to wane

Disembodied headlights
Dart between the trees
The car speeds on to sanctuary
It carries day-time's refugees

Pilgrim beacons flicker
From aircraft as they fly
As hopes and fears and gain and loss
Pass through the velvet sky

A horizon-chasing satellite
Glints metallic on its spree
A prisoner of gravity
But so, again, are we

And far away in time and space
Shimmers the Milky Way
I look back and wonder
A cosmic castaway

I see the nightlight now
Pale yellow in the hall
I see the shadow of our bed
Dancing on the wall

And we will sleep together
Now this day is done
Nightlights will surround us
Until Lucifer brings the sun

Spells of Life and Growth

I AM

I am a shadow
Between darkness and light
A suggestion of movement
I shimmer and fade
Between darkness and light
At the edge of your sight

I am the perfume
Within the night air
A memory blooms
As I float through your mind
Within the night air
A scent subtle and rare

I am a whisper
Beneath all the din
A musical voice
That pleads to be heard

Beneath all the din
If you let me in

I am sweetness
Hidden in sour
A promise of something
Something you need
Hidden in sour
Like a thorn with a flower

I am the embrace
You might yet know
A soft feather touch
A thrill to your soul
You might yet know
If you don't let me go

A PITCH IN TIME

Back from commercial and somehow
The runner must move along
Third is deep, he looks asleep
The fielder's position is wrong

This guy was a standout in Triple A
Great strength swinging the bat
Time! The catcher is out to the mound
Now he and the pitcher will chat

With a runner on second they're changing the calls
Deciding what's best for this hitter
They'll probably opt to go with the curve
He's had trouble controlling the splitter

I love how he works and he's got good stuff
But he's cooled off a little of late
His mechanics seem sound but his problem has been
Leaving fastballs belt-high at the plate

The batter completed his studies at Yale
Alpha Epsilon Pi
I bet he knows the Latin for Blue Jays
Is Cyanocittae Cristatae

His father played winter ball down in San Juan
A base-stealer, played centre field
He hurt himself badly sliding to home
And he never completely healed

Looks like he has the old man's speed
But he needs to grind this one out
With an open roof on this humid night
The ball is darting about

There's a hot dog promotion in Section D
A Loonie each just for today
Chilli and cheese included, of course
It looks like we're ready to play

The batter squares up, here comes the pitch
Popped up to the shortstop out front
And now, another word from our sponsor
What a poor, poor attempt at a bunt

POETIC

Poetic symbols
The urge for verse
English á la mode
Whether sonnet or ode
For rhyme or worse!

As words elucidate
And exhilarate
They resonate
Poetic

When I manipulate
And articulate
In decipherable code
Sensations explode
Planned or extemporized
Poetic

BERTHA THOMPSON[1]

She misplaced her needle when quilting one night
So picked up her pen and started to write
The words came so quickly, she wanted to share
Thoughts from the parlour and the old rocking chair

The drive lined with flowers and rocks painted white
Led to a window of flickering light
At the worn kitchen table, cleared of its mess
Bertha would sit in her flower-print dress

And from her memory pictures would flow
Of children, and nature, and times long ago
Her pen weaved a spell as she sat in this nook
As people and scenes came alive in her book

She prayed for protection when darkness came on
And gave thanks to God at the breaking of dawn
In the roar of the wind, the scent of a flower
Bertha could feel there existed a power

She baked with ice cream when the milk had run out
Her sugary tea was the best, beyond doubt
Cookies for little ones and crumbs for the birds
The substance of living she sweetened with words

She wrote of her times as girl, mother, and wife
Of duties and chores that were part of her life
Managed the house, raised three girls and three boys
She worked like the dickens and worked without noise

Bertha captured the joy of birds in the spring
The sights and the sounds that the seasons can bring
She knew the fall colours, the wind's icy chill
And set her thoughts down when the evening was still

She told of the green grass, the buzzing of bees
Of crops and of meadows, of rivers and trees
She wrote of small wonders, she set them to rhyme
It helped to stay busy and make use of her time

Bertha saw diamonds in the morning's bright dew
She spoke from her heart so her words would ring true

She told her stories; she was able to share
Thoughts from the parlour and her old rocking chair

---

[1] Bertha Thompson of Milltown Cross and Montague began writing at the age of 83: "I just happened to lose my sewing needle one night and I picked up a pen." Her first poem, *I Hear a Robin. I Hear a Blue Jay,* was published in an Island seniors' magazine. Two other poems were published in the USA. Bertha's honest verse is true folk-poetry. She died in 1999, aged 89.

IT'S PROBABLY LOVE

It looks like the gleam in Grandmother's eye
Received as a gift that no-one could buy
It shines in the morning, bright with the sun
And lasts through the evening when the day's done

It tastes like that hot dog, shared with your dad
Around the campfire when you were a lad
The savour of root beer on your first date
The promise of sweetness that may await

It smells like that dinner, cooked with a friend
Or the flowers you remembered to send
The fragrance it has is like her perfume
Or a walk on the trail where roses bloom

It sounds like the whisper that calmed your fear
A sob or a laugh when comfort is near

It is the hush in the spaces between
Music that followed wherever you'd been

It feels like the hug when we said *Goodbye*
Soft as the tissue when you wiped your eye
As firm as the grip that helped you to stand
And primal, like walking barefoot in the sand

It's inside and out, below and above
Life's better with it; it's probably love

P.E.I. NATIONAL PARK

In the wilds of P.E.I. National Park
Stay alert in the daytime, take care after dark

The plovers will warn you with whistles and peeps
Before they attack with razor-sharp beaks
A beaver appears as meek as a lamb
Then will turn savage and not give a damn
Stay clear of red squirrels: to confront them takes guts
They seethe with menace if you threaten their nuts
Hares may love running and leaping about
Be warned: their rear feet can give you a clout
Stay off the dunes: don't risk your life
For marram grass fronds cut like a knife
Watch where you step, stay clear of small holes
Lest you be mobbed by an army of voles
The marsh harbours creatures of dark, ill repute
For many a tourist fell afoul of a newt
Out on the beach you may feel a jab
And discover you've lost a toe to a crab

Most fearsome of all: the Souvenir Clan
They'll ply you with dolls of their red-haired God: Anne

So, please, dear Visitor, before you embark
Beware, yes, beware of P.E.I. National Park!

TOMMY'S PLACE

There's a place where Tommy hides
With brittle-leafed October trees
Branches cling and scratch his arms
Mossy ground stains his knees

There the child considers things
Like crunchy leaves and sweet fall air
His brown eyes peer about the woods
Beneath a fringe of thick, dark hair

He's been there many times since spring
And watched the summer come and go
April's only six months past
But seems a thousand years ago

For six months now he's watched the birds
Build nests and raise their rowdy broods
The chicks grew strong and now they've left
For life in warmer latitudes

He's heard the bullfrog's solemn note
He's heard the osprey's piercing cry
He's smelled the chestnut's heady scent
He's watched as flowers bloom and die

Sometimes, Tommy's mind lies quiet
Mirrored in this sacred space
There's no one here to question him
Or read what's written on his face

Tommy feels he might be waiting
For whom or what he's just not sure
Will a stranger visit him
Or is it one he's known before?

In brittle-leafed October trees
Will Tommy hear his mother call?
This is the place where Tommy hides
It's just a place, that's all

PLANETARY CONJUNCTION

In the ocean of night
Planets align
And appear as one light

Far apart in their flight
The shimmer combines
In the ocean of night

A point burnt on our sight
Though distant they shine
Yet appear as one light

On the black southern height
Stands the heavenly sign
In the ocean of night

Celestial delight
That is both yours and mine
Now appears as one light

Eerily bright
Sacred design
In the ocean of night
They appear as one light

WOODLAND CONVERSATION

Give me one of your chicks, Crow
I am hungry
The weakling will die before
Leaf buds adorn trees
Time is wasted on the fated
Give him to me

He may see the leaves, Fox
And fights to live
Weak ones may grow in feather
If Creator wills
The brood is not diminished
He may live on

My kits squabble in the den
And cry for food
Throw the boisterous chick for she
Claims the nest

And will usurp her parents' power
Give her to me

She may find the certain path
That rules the wood
They grow brave, that are guided
True in the murder
Her journey just begins
With beak and claw

Crow, I will bark at the moon
And curse your name
For the earth clan will prevail
With fur and fang
And fill our store in clay dens
Amid the roots

Fox, I shall soar to the moon
And shade her glow
The nest will hide in shadow
While we call above
Feathered kind remains unafraid
Until you fly

FALL MIGRATION

My spirit soars
When I see geese take flight
Upon their pilgrimage
To seek the light

From James Bay shores
Where dynasties fight
Over sacred ancestral dust

To Tallahassee marshes
Where they alight
On the warm, sub-tropic gust

(Between
Is the journey
Fuelled by subconscious longing
Shepherded by unanointed leaders
Guided by race memory
Accompanied by plaintive music

While I remain
The ancient idea flies above
Free of borders
An entity of instinctual purpose
Carving the air
Home on the empyrean highway
For home moves with the flock
As wing beat follows wing beat
Into another's horizon)

My soul is freed
When geese take flight
In Vs and echelons
To seek the light

ISLAND JUNE

The woodland Lady's Slipper blushes pink
Coruscating streams dance on the shoals
Just now the tourists flow across the link
Their racing minds alive with summer goals
Summer friends are welcomed back again
We ride the rolling wave their presence brings
Remembering our red-clay land's allure
The hymnals out and everybody sings
Let storefronts ring out to the tune of gain
The farmer lives in hope of evening rain
And orchids still endure

MERMAID'S KISS

I fall into your music
As it tumbles ashore
It ebbs and it flows
And I need to hear more

But under the tune
Floats an ominous sound
Like echoes from caverns
Far underground

You gaze in your pool
Combing your hair
And your grey eyes look back
With a blank, soulless stare

Do you think of your lover
And the cruelty of fate?
Do you remember the loss?
How long must you wait?

Sublime, hollow woman
Swim me below
Through canyons and forests
Where cold currents flow

As the moon weeps
Take me to the abyss
I'll die in your ocean
For your mermaid's kiss

RED LEAF IN SEPTEMBER

Stay
Your sisters dance, green upon the bough
Why forsake easy-warm summer?
The aster yet blooms pink
The berry-ripening moon is just past
Endure, until certain autumn commands the end of days

I drank light and air
Unfolded to the sky
And spilled my energy, free with joy
I shall not cling, withered in the paling sun
Before the long shadow creeps
Let me blaze and fall

WEEDS

We have to bend our backs
When we plant the seeds
Before the autumn harvest
We must pull the weeds

Tansey ragwort thrived here
Before we tilled this land
But it has no place
Now the garden's planned

Penny cress and pepper grass
Danced where the west wind blows
They can stay along the edges
But we'll pluck them from the rows

Ox-eyed daisy and shepherd's purse
Swayed amid the fields
We must uproot them from the drills
Lest they harm our yields

Some may forage in the woodland
That could meet their needs
But when we grow our garden
We must pull the weeds

REDPOLL

The redpoll danced around the seed and flew
I didn't see the bright red cap again
Away to better food or something new
To search the neighbourhood for fresher grain

Pink breasted nomad down from Hudson Bay
You find my choice of food not to your taste?
I thought the sunflower seeds would make you stay
A feast unknown in your subarctic waste
I never thought to yield to your conceit
I fed you like an ordinary bird
I'm shocked to find you part of an elite
A blue blood, not of the common herd

I welcome whomsoever nature sends
Content to number chickadees as friends

PHOTOSYNTHESIS

Energy travels as quanta of light
From ninety-three million miles away
The leaf absorbs unlimited amounts
(I assume, of course, it's a sunny day)

Sunlight is drunk by chlorophyll
Enclosed in the cytoplasm of a cell
Because plants are complex organisms
In the leaves: that's where the chloroplasts dwell

The water and carbon dioxide react
Thereby creating something quite new
Glucose remains, oxygen released
$C_6H_{12}0_6$ plus 60_2

So *Thank you* cyanobacteria bloom
Without you we'd be comprehensively doomed!

A CRACK AMID THE STONE

The concrete slab is whiter than a bone
As cold and unforgiving as the grave
Yet flowers may find a crack amid the stone

The city wind howls, power wires moan
And footsteps echo; it sounds like a cave
Where concrete lies, dull, whiter than a bone

Grey puddles splash, your body pushed and blown
Along the sidewalk while you long and crave
For flowers to find a crack amid the stone

The trees stand stark and all the birds are flown
And down the parkland trails you find that they've
Set concrete paths now, whiter than a bone

The diesel reeks. Uncertainty is sown
But when you walk, tread lightly: you can save
The flowers that find a crack amid the stone

Through noisy city streets you walk alone
And the monster has taken all you gave
Though concrete slabs are whiter than a bone
Some flowers have found a crack amid the stone

TOWARD THE LIGHT

A crocus never lasts to see a rose
But blooms and fades before the end of spring
A short and empty lifespan, I suppose
Lived out while frosts still bite and north winds sting
Too soon to join with nature in her prime
An unambitious flower of little worth
Shall I remember you come summertime
When perfumed, painted gardens carpet Earth?
And yet you lead us back toward the light
Foretell the coming warmth and lengthening days
Defy the creeping grasp of winter's night
And herald hope and growth in vibrant May
A full and worthy sojourn, I propose
Although you never live to see a rose

Spells of the Spirit

HAUNTED

I hear the wind, relentless, at my door
It clamours now, demands I stay awake
And rattles as it never has before

My thoughts careen and dive as if to take
A path that's independent of my mind
And conjure punishments for my mistake

The phantom wind, the phantom thoughts, unkind
Like inky whirlpools spin into the night
And bury hope and peace too deep to find

Shall I rejoice to see the morning light?
Are demons exorcised at break of day?
Do shadows live, although the sun shines bright?

I shall not be haunted, evermore
The wind has travelled onward from my door

FOUR TANKAS

I watch the storm waves
Invade and tear at the sand
And the shore is changed
Paths never to be restored
But new ways to walk upon

Distant stars burn on
Jewels to brighten our nights
Impossibly far
Now, let us light our candles
Each a star to the other

I smell the fall leaves
See bright colours of decay
And mourn the passing
Then wait with coat drawn closely
In hope of resurrection

You walked on my left
Footsteps crunched the gravel trail
Now I step alone
Beside me an empty space
I'm free to tread either side

HEXED AND VEXED

She eats Froot Loops from a cauldron
Travels to work on a broom
She talks to the cat
The cat talks back
Under the light of the moon

On Sunday she heads to the coven
While I make tea at home
They all drop in after
Weird cackles and laughter
And her mother is quite the old crone

She really is an enchantress
Where she's going I never can tell
And, if I ask
She tells me, *Relax*
I'm just going out for a spell

I know we have separate interests
And I don't want to be an old grouch
But when her boss comes to call
He leaves his horns in the hall
And puts his hooves up on the couch

We attended a function last weekend
She asked me to be the emcee
Strange creatures came
They had curious names
But none seemed familiar to me

I'd like to see other people
But there could be a hitch
I may be changed
Have my limbs rearranged
I fear I'm dating a... witch

MAGUS

We've journeyed together over the years
Since the asphalt river engulfed our clay stream
Shared sparkling joys and grey, leaden fears
Died the same nightmare, lived the same dream
Rain on the window reflected your tears
The white line leapt on in the headlights' cool gleam
Flying above us, the all-knowing moon
Please, pass me my gold; my bus stop is soon

Many a pilgrim stepped on or alit
Most passed like ghosts on the edge of our sight
Some we missed more than we will admit
Whose company brought us a world of delight
And I recall one who sat where you sit
Her laughter and smile brightened the night
I could remain with you but, I think, instead
My frankincense, please; my stop is ahead

I'm leaving my seat and this is *Goodbye*
The driveway looms long and dark up ahead
That I have loved you, I cannot deny
But now is the time to bury our dead
Ask me no questions, I can't answer *Why*
All I will leave is my echoing tread
The bus is now slowing, I'll soon be gone
I'll just take my myrrh now; I must move on

SPRING ON CONNOLLY STREET

From Value Village and across the broken parking lot
(The pot-holed and rippled asphalt at low tide)
The car nods and hisses through puddles that reflect slate clouds
Soggy Tim Horton's cups decorate the defeated gutter snow

The car rolls through the stop sign
And staggers up the curb
Hanging on a bulging tyre
Hopeful sunlight glints on the windshield

Persephone returns to the awakened world?
Or the Missus dropped off at the bingo

VISIT TO MANHATTAN

Mary pulls her shopping cart
On Broadway, Upper West Side
She ignores the crosswalk light
Looking neither left nor right
Gliding between the cars
On Broadway, Upper West Side
She can sense the traffic flow
Taxis jolting to and fro
Honking loudly all the while
On Broadway, Upper West Side

A cab driver speeds his fare
To Times Square, hub of Midtown
Billboards light the clubs and bars
Pixels shine instead of stars
They glare high above us
On Times Square, hub of Midtown
Naked mimes and tourists clash
Vendors take out evening trash

To the curbs of side streets
On Times Square, hub of Midtown

People push and bump along
In the streets of Downtown
Buses, cars, and subways roar
Concrete forests reach and soar
To obscure the night sky
In the streets of Downtown
Picture windows look on out
Down below the sirens shout
Cutting through the night air
In the streets of Downtown

Where twin towers used to stand
And fate galvanised this land
That Mary still calls home

ANTECEDENTS

The tree gains substance from the sun and rain
And stretches thankful branches out to God
A forest track becomes a country lane
And tourists stroll where forbears roamed, unshod
My memory is older than my mind
I understand the debt I owe the past
I see how thought and action are refined
I know that worthy words and art will last
Although you're gone, our conversation flows
Your spirit speaks, now, from that distant age
I borrow your ideas, which I transpose
And let them live, again, upon my page
The tree drinks deep through strong, ancestral roots
And I, who tend the orchard, reap the fruits

THE SONG

My Love, I fear that we lack harmony
The summer tune is warm, and full, and lush
Yet you play nothing but the minor key
Your last note dwindles to a pensive hush
We all keep time, gracefully, as one
While there you sit: detached, a soul alone
We dance in light but you avoid the sun
And add a dark, unwanted, sombre tone
The echo of the bell is always there
And through the ages we hear it resound
But we can climb out of this pit of care
To blend our voices in a joyful sound!
The future and the past are out of sight
So, please, don't sing unhappy songs tonight

PROMETHEUS

An offering of trees consigned to flame
The alchemy of wood and air and spark
Allowing us to reach out in the dark
To subjugate and render nature tame

The burning standard leads the armies on
And victory comes either late or soon
White radiance is reflected in the moon
And blazes out its glory to the sun

We stumble on with unrestrained desire
The history of all is that of fire

NOWHERE WINDS (MAURICE WILSON)[2]

Here, in dawn's redeeming light
I hear a summons from far away
A call to scale the sacred height
Without excuse. Without delay
So start the engine, make the flight
Even if there's Hell to pay
I'm the lamp to pierce the night
This is my hour, today's the day
Just one more dragon left to slay
God shakes the tree, one leaf falls
On a crag, a raven calls

I hold my gun at Passchendaele
(An orphan from a widows' town
Where grey men drink of bitter ale)
I see boys left in mud to drown
And tear through life's too fragile veil
As gas rolls in like Death's own gown
How is it that I prevail?

While sunlight oozes, sticky brown
With nowhere else to go but down
God shakes the tree, one leaf falls
On a crag, a raven calls

The voice of silence fills the sky
It holds a meaning I can't know
My tears freeze instantly I cry
In the nowhere winds that blow
And no one's ever climbed this high
Lost memories wait down below
I've died before, again I die
My comrades rise from long ago
They gather around me in the snow
God shakes the tree, one leaf falls
On a crag, a raven calls

---

[2] For further information on Maurice Wilson see *The Moth and the Mountain* by Ed Caesar (Simon & Schuster, 2020).

IF WE HAD KNOWN

What would have changed if we had known
And waited for wind and tide to shift?
Waited, and not moved alone
What would have changed if we had known
Together rather than alone
Tethered was better than adrift?
What would have changed if we had known
And waited for wind and tide to shift?

SPELLS AGAINST THE DARKNESS[3]

Farewell to passing daylight
Here in twilight
Birds call out their evensong
When too-heavy sun falls from sight
Colours fade, all is pale
Clouds become a smoky veil
Here in twilight

Darkness falls across the sea
Faint stars shine
The barn owl settles in the tree
Moonlight shimmers through the pine
A warm breeze reaches to caress
And whispers spells against the darkness
As faint stars shine

---

[3] "Spells Against the Darkness" is inspired by a phrase from Roger McGough's foreword to the poetry anthology *Poetry, Please* (Faber & Faber, 2013): "...Poetry is an affirmation of joy and a spell against the dark."

ALICE

Here you sit, Mrs. Hargreaves
With octogenarian consciousness
And listen to the New Forest leaves

Eyes reflected in the study window
Once cried tears for your dead soldier sons
And held the gaze of European royalty

Hunter's eyes burned from the face of the sepia goddess
Just twenty years old with wild, dark hair

Innocent eyes opened wide at the telling of the story

They close now and see past Julys, sunny skies, and the river
When you were Alice

1972

I'm stuck in nineteen seventy-two
There's definitely something wrong
A tragic affliction, strange but true

I'm repulsed by all that's new
I like to play Atari Pong
I'm stuck in nineteen seventy-two

My friends number very few
"Greased Lightning" is my favourite song
A tragic affliction, strange but true

About current trends I haven't a clue
I wear platform soles; is that wrong?
I'm stuck in nineteen seventy-two

I drive an AMC Gremlin too
And strike my Hare Krishna gong
A tragic affliction, strange but true

I feel that problems may ensue
But I'll stay Barbra-Streisand strong
I'm stuck in nineteen seventy-two
A tragic affliction, strange but true

PILGRIM

From the mud and clinging swamp, I clawed free
On the mount of tumbling certainty, I kept my poise
I fled the flattering city as a refugee
I outwitted the deceitful forest and all its ploys
I leapt the idiot river and its tyranny of noise
I'm sadder now, after all the paths I've trod
If you call me Pilgrim, I will call you God

EDEN FELL

I grow with twisted branches on this hill
They reach the sky, my roots delve into Hell
And through the tumbling centuries you will
Hear the echo from when Eden fell
As from naivety you came awake
When Eve was wise enough to hear a snake
My knowledge colours every tale you tell
My stirrings, every thought your mind conceives
Your breath a fading breeze that rattles through my leaves

Spells for Peace

SOURIS LINE ROAD

Unsure of your directions
When far from your abode?
There's a place that points from south to north
It's called the Souris Line Road

When you find yourself frustrated
And you think you might explode
We have windmills you can tilt at
Down the Souris Line Road

If you feel confined and breathless
And need to shed your load
Fields roll on forever
Along the Souris Line Road

Speaking with your children
But they seem to talk in code?
Everything makes perfect sense
Here on the Souris Line Road

Tired of regulations
And lines that must be toed?
Come, lose yourself deep in the woods
At the Souris Line Road

Your nose is to the grindstone
There's money that is owed
But trout are in MacInnis's Pond
Up the Souris Line Road

So, when you find life's show is stuck
On a dreary episode
Turn it off and switch on here
Out on the Souris Line Road

UNSOLICITED ADVICE

Don't fear tomorrow: live your life today
Your actions, now, redeem the coming years
Follow your heart. Run wild but not astray

Go seek the sun. Dance in the light of day
Be deaf to those who throw embarrassed jeers
Don't fear tomorrow: live your life today

No need to please another: it's okay
Be wary of the superficial cheers
Follow your heart. Run wild but not astray

Remember you are human, made of clay
Yet smiles are found within this vale of tears
Don't fear tomorrow: live your life today

When you sense God's presence, stop and pray
But carefully deflect religion's spears
Follow your heart. Run wild but not astray

Believe yourself. Don't give your soul away
The Kingdom is for those who persevere
Don't fear tomorrow: live your life today
Follow your heart. Run wild but not astray

JESUS OF NAZARETH

Jesus of Nazareth, tell me what's new
Crack open time and wait by the shore
Open the moment and lead me on through

We'll paddle around Galilee in my canoe
With you aboard, I'll feel secure
Jesus of Nazareth, tell me what's new

See you in Cana with all your crew
Make some good wine and pour me the cure
Open the moment and lead me on through

Over in Bethany we'll rendezvous
With Mary and Martha, a table for four
Jesus of Nazareth, tell me what's new

Let's see the sights, there's so much to do
Looking for answers, I'll knock on the door
Open the moment and lead me on through

Thanks a lot, Jesus; merci beaucoup
God, man, and myth; the stories endure
Jesus of Nazareth, tell me what's new
Open the moment and lead me on through

THE FRONT WINDOW

As April's evening fades into the west
Cold shadows stretch out, long, across the grass
An eagle carries twigs to build her nest
Reflected in the river, just like glass
A crocus reaches skyward from the earth
Last vestiges of snow melt in the air
Small birds sing out sweet songs for all they're worth
Of human troubles they are unaware
As winter's ebb gives way to summer's flow
My window frames this ever-changing scene
A promise seems to live in sundown's glow
That what was dead and grey will flood with green
Stand here with me. Look out across the park
And understand that dawn will follow dark

RIDING HIGH

Each pedal stroke a click of the prayer beads
Pilgrimage spun out across the pavement
Joyous movement cries to Heaven

Hallowed be Thy name, God of bicycles
Deliver us from the shortcut
Strengthen us to meet incline and headwind

Praise for laboured breath and burning thighs
We fly like angels on high
Road without end. Amen

YELLOW GIRAFFE

Grayson, where's your yellow giraffe?
It's your favourite toy of all
Show it to the daycare staff
Grayson, find your yellow giraffe
Chew it hard and make us laugh
If we've misplaced it, you will bawl
Grayson hug your yellow giraffe
It's your favourite toy of all

FERRY-WISE

The parking lot at Caribou is cracked and faded grey
And the Holiday Island ferry is entering the bay
Ten minutes 'til she gets here, twenty more 'til we can load
Then an hour and a half before I hit a red dirt road

But I'm already home
We're driving through the night
Driving nowhere special
With just the moon for light

The vehicle deck is crowded and reeks of diesel fumes
Rusted steel and bolts and rivets decorate the gloom
Puddled, paint-peeled walkways lead to metal stairs above
An hour and a quarter, then I'm with the one I love

But I'm already home
With you on the sand
We look out on the ocean
And walk on, hand in hand

Plastic chairs and tables bear the scars of years
Semi-opaque windows wear salty spray like tears
A change of course and rising swell bring on a jarring shake
Thirty minutes now will end this homesick ache

But I'm already home
I bask in friendly smiles
Anchored on your back deck
No more lonely miles

Travel-weary voyagers are milling round the stairs
TVs crackle static while the PA system blares
The final shudder tells me that we're mooring at the pier
Hydraulic hiss and starting cars; my journey's end is near

But I'm already home
I never went away
Although Fate has tried its best
Enticing me to stray

I'm already home
Beneath the Island sky
Determined to stay
And never say *Goodbye*

BABY

The sky is dark. Stars are shining
Your eyes are dark. What do you see?
Can you see new joys unfolding
As you stare deep into me?

You can watch the Earth revealing
Rocky peaks and the Island sea
The sky is dark. Stars are shining
Your eyes are dark. What do you see?

Every moment new stars appearing
Worlds that have been or yet to be
Now you smile with unfettered feeling
Your eyes are the night sky, what do you see?

BAPTISM

I lie in my Jordan
Clouded with magnesium salts
And meditate upon my faults
Not envy, that is numbed by age
I've read on past that well-thumbed page

Amid the bubbles
That froth and cling against my skin
I ponder how to cleanse my sin
Not greed, I think from my acrylic font
I own more than I could ever want

Cocooned
While warm water laps
And thoughts cascade as if from taps
Not pride. I know my place on Earth
My inconsequence and worth

Through the steam
As droplets coalesce and plunge
What use to me the scouring sponge?
Yes! Sloth. The horror of wasted time
Theft of hours: unanswerable crime!

I emerge, reborn
A bar of Dove falls from the shelf
I've washed away my former self
To plan and act is now my fate
I have atoned. My path is straight

TIM'S HOUSE

People rush too much
I prefer steady and slow
When renovating and such

I'll realize the vision although
I don't crack on apace
And, perhaps, there's little to show

I'm making this small house my place
In my way; not too fast
I'll not run another's race

This is built to last
From sculpted corbel to cast iron sink
Hope for my future, built on the past

People rush too much, I think

I'll conduct a symphony of wood
While I gaze at the fan-lit front door
Proportions stand as they should

Ratio exact; neither less nor more
A gem to delight
From back extension to refinished floor

Windows glance, in daylight
To the step where I sit and sing
And the house number is painted bright

Here you'll find me in the evening
And you may hear a wine glass clink
Hurrying is not my thing

People rush too much, I think

LEGACY

I planted a straight, sturdy oak sapling
As a legacy (and in remembrance)
The north wind
Blew: ice, salt, and bitterness
Sung a harsh, frozen challenge
Others of the glade fell

The oak swayed and bent in the blast
Stunted and scarred to windward
Striving in desperate asymmetry
Cracked and moss-scabbed
No more a sapling
Defiant and bent against the sky

MIRROR MOON

Do you hear the water song?
It rises from the evening river
Do you hear enchantments spoken
In the gloaming, still and holy?
And the light subtle, gold
Reflected in the mirror moon

In the depths, floats the moon
It shimmers to the stains of song
While spirit traces grey and gold
Haunt the surface of the river
And night owls chant holy
Words that cling to mist as they are spoken

Stories of the night are spoken
Beneath the gaze of Princess Moon
Who shines on the profane and holy
Breathes memories into the song

Memories of the ancient river
Weeping from the eye of gold

Here lies the past as heavy gold
And the prayers are spoken
Humbly, at the altar of the river
As branches stir across the moon
Then the piper plays his song
Sanctifies, and all is holy

Willows mark the holy
Ground, rushes bow their heads of gold
And between the lines of song
Hear words of deeper learning spoken
Through cobalt clouds, the prodigal moon
Bestows her light upon the river

Dream and gaze into the river
Where mist plumes rise like holy
Incense, in service to the goddess moon
Now the horizon is tinged with gold
Hear the prayers of morning spoken
And a new voice fills the song

Resurrected holy dawn bleeds gold
As the moon fades in the river
And poems are spoken beneath the song

SOMETIMES IT SNOWS IN APRIL

Sometimes it snows in April
Though we hope that warmth will stay
Defeated, we rediscover
Coats we'd stored away
The wind cries from the east
Grey clouds choke the skies
Sometimes it snows in April
And the cold wind stings our eyes

Blythe promises of springtime
Lie buried in the cold
Love we felt on sun-filled days
Seems remote and old
We avoid each other's glances
And leave an awkward space to fill
Sometimes it snows in April
Now we languish in the chill

The snow and ice will melt
(So turns the wheel of fate)
We know that flowers will bloom again
For us it may be too late
The fickle, lying calendar
Won't tell us what is true
Sometimes it snows in April
And there's nothing we can do

LOST SAPLING

I trimmed you only to increase your strength
So you'd grow straight and not break in the gust
I felt that I would go to any length
To keep you free from canker, rot, and rust
I watered deep and met your sapling needs
But left you space enough to feel the sun
I ruthlessly dug out encroaching weeds
Ensuring that you'd not be overrun
In truth, you now stand solid, trunk and root
And independent of my watchful eye
Your flowers dazzle, boughs cascade with fruit
Your leaves, like waves, beneath the forest sky
I fear the day approaches when I should
Not recognize my sapling in the wood

About the Author

Born in Melton Mowbray, England, Roderick MacDonald is a 40-year resident of Prince Edward Island. He has volunteered with several community and sport organizations. *Spells Against the Darkness* is his second book of poetry. MacDonald is happiest on the shorelines or in the countryside near the village of Morell, where he lives with his wife.